LeBron James: The Inspiring Story of One of Basketball's Greatest Players

An Unauthorized Biography

By: Clayton Geoffreys

Table of Contents

Foreword

Every few decades, a player enters the league and completely changes the game. LeBron James has been one of those players. Easily considered one of the most versatile players in basketball today, LeBron has established a name brand for himself among players, fans, and NBA owners. There are few players who can truly hold the title of franchise player—LeBron is one of those players. LeBron's journey has been intensely followed. Fans have been able to watch a once young man coming right out of high school grow into a dominant leader and motivator on and off the court. Around the league, LeBron has grown to demand as much respect as other greats like Kobe Bryant. Thank you for downloading *LeBron James: The Inspiring Story of One of Basketball's Greatest Players*. In this unauthorized biography, we will learn LeBron's incredible life story and impact on the game of basketball. Hope you enjoy and if you do, please do not forget to leave a review! Also, check out my website at <u>claytongeoffreys.com</u> to join my exclusive list where I let you know about my latest books and give you goodies!

Cheers,

Clayton Geoffreys

Visit me at <u>www.claytongeoffreys.com</u>

Introduction

LeBron James is a basketball player whose talent was home grown in the city of Akron, Ohio. Currently he is the unquestioned leader of the Cleveland Cavaliers and one of the most respected icons of sports history, James has accomplished great feats in a decade as a professional basketball player. A two-time NBA Champion with the Miami Heat, LeBron has received the Finals MVP twice, and assembled a collection of four MVP trophies. A complete cleaner on the stat sheet, James has also led in the intangible areas of the game, specifically on the defensive end. LeBron has been a member of the All Defensive First Team for five years. People all around the world recognize his legendary persona. His current mission is to bring a title to his championship-deprived city of Cleveland.

James is an international icon. In the business world, James has established himself as one of the powerhouse figures in sports marketing through his basketball play. The LeBron James brand is one of the most valuable in terms of sports branding. According to Forbes, James surpassed Tiger Woods in being one of the most valuable sports names in the world.

His game, like his physical build, is something the world has never seen before. At an incredible 6' 9", James showed the ability to run the floor with a guard-like poise. Prior to the 2004 NBA season, the NBA and its fans never saw a specimen like James. Everything from his biological make-up to his ability to understand the game in a cerebral way seemed to be a manifestation of what was only created by a basketball god. Contrary to what his doubters would have liked, LeBron appeared to seamlessly transition from his high school style of play into the NBA. His all-around ability to rebound, to dish to his teammates for an easy basket, and to devastate teams around the rim has never wavered, even as the talent around the league has improved over the years.

Driving to the rim, James is simply a beast. With his 250-pound frame, even the best one-on-one defenders have a hard time guarding LeBron. Teams like San Antonio come up with comprehensive scouting reports to stop James. As if his athleticism wasn't enough, LeBron is like a basketball professor. Through his willingness to listen and probe the minds of his coaches, LeBron funnels all of his physical talent into showing fans a basketball savant displayed through his artistry. Not only is his athleticism used to make himself better; he impacts the game in unprecedented ways to elevate his team.

When off the court hanging with friends and family, LeBron James is a joker. Unlike the endless amount of quiet and grounded egos like Kevin Durant, Damian Lillard, and Derrick Rose, James is an extroverted leader, and not afraid to crack a joke. Friends of LeBron were quick to respond to reporters when they mentioned LeBron's comedic abilities. One friend, Randy Mims, said that there's "sheer laughter" from morning until sundown. As a loud and vocal leader, LeBron makes himself heard whether he is on the court leading his team, or supporting on the sidelines. Another distinct characteristic of LeBron is his ability to balance the scales of showmanship and humility. Despite his perceived perfection, James has made many mistakes over his public career. Given his circumstances, he has stood out compared to other athletes in being humble despite his outgoing demeanor.

In spite of his superstar status, LeBron has had his fair share of personal struggles. Being raised by a single teenage mother, LeBron encountered poverty, lived through sub-optimal conditions, and suffered through emotional struggles. Those personal struggles are frequently linked to the absence of James' father in his life. These elements in James' story are what give him his humility. His godlike talent on the court is balanced by his humble beginnings, which allows for fans to relate to him on a human level.

Currently as of early 2015, LeBron is the co-captain of a heavily scrutinized Cavaliers team looking to contend for titles.

Chapter 1: Childhood and Early Life

As a child, the iconic Little Tikes hoop that many kids had growing up cultivated LeBron's love for the game. In numerous interviews, his mother Gloria recalls the infant James dunking on the staple household item. Little did she know that this planted a seed in James' mind to strive to become one of the most iconic athletes ever.

In his toddler years, James and his mother lived with their grandmother. This gave James a semblance of a normal childhood for many years. However, the passing of his grandmother marked the beginning of a new struggle for Gloria James and her only son. Gloria and her brothers could not pay bills, leading to no water, heat and other living necessities. They would get by with government assistance as well as the help of neighbors and friends. Moving from apartment to house to apartment was something that James had to get used to as a child.

James envied his friends who had fathers. In an interview, he stated that, "Not having that father figure around was difficult when I went to some of my friends' houses, because they had their fathers and mothers around."

A theme in James' early life was receiving assistance outside of his family. The James family started finding some security again when a local football coach took James under his wing. Bruce Kelker was in search of players for his football team. Stunned by the speed and athleticism the nine-year-old James displayed, Kelker wanted James on his team. After realizing the living conditions the James family was going through, Kelker took in Gloria and LeBron to live in with them.

The next coach to support the James family was Frankie Walker, who was a middle school basketball coach. It was with Walker that James learned the value of discipline by completing chores and finishing homework on a routine basis. Prior to Walker, James missed many school classes. That all changed with the new values Walker tried to implement in James.

In middle school, James would play for the Ohio Shooting Stars, an AAU team organized by Dru Joyce, the father of his friend, Dru Joyce II. This was where the famed Fab 4 were established and where the rise of James' basketball skills took off. The core made it to the AAU Finals, but they would ultimately narrowly lose. James would miss the buzzer-beating shot to win the game. James and his new best friends formed an extremely close bond over the ups and downs of trying to win the AAU title that summer. They all made a promise to each other to play on the same high school basketball team.

Chapter 2: High School Years

LeBron underwent an evolution in his humanity during his high school years. His meteoric rise to basketball stardom was a huge change for him. The fame that ran parallel to his ascent in basketball was something LeBron never had dealt with before. The type of life experiences he encountered set him apart from any teenager growing up in the United States.

Freshman Year – Buchtel or Saint Vincent-Saint Mary

James and his three AAU teammates and best friends, Sian Cotton, Dru Joyce II and Willie were headed to Saint Vincent-Saint Mary High School for their remaining four years of education and basketball. It was a controversial choice at the time because there was an unwritten rule in Akron that black kids usually went to Buchtel. In Akron, if you were black, you went to Buchtel, and if you were white, you went to St. Vincent St. Mary. SVSM was practically an all-white school. It was LeBron's long-time friend, Dru Joyce II, who would change their high school destination. Before making a decision, Dru Joyce developed a close relationship with Keith Dambrot, the coach of SVSM's basketball team. Joyce never seemed to get the growth spurt his friends got, and he wasn't able to gain the respect he wanted from the Buchtel coach. He saw no hope in receiving minutes on the court. That changed with Dambrot, who saw heart and a fiery passion bursting from Joyce. Joyce's short stature was not a hindrance to the SVSM coach. With the promise of playing time if he kept up his work ethic, Joyce opted to go to SVSM. LeBron, Sian, and Willie did only what felt right in their hearts, which was to follow their best friend.

SVSM surprised other high schools not only with their talent, but their main rotation of seven players consisted of four freshman. It was no surprise to LeBron and his Fab 4 crew. It was a project in the making for a few years in middle school, so the team chemistry was already established. LeBron's desire to make other players benefit from his talent was also a huge factor. Many high school players seek to buff their points and be the go-to guy, but LeBron was extremely different in that regard. Dambrot recalled an incident where James deferred from taking the last shot to win the game to set up for a better shot by passing off to a teammate. From a young age, James was taught that basketball is a team sport, and it manifested through his ability to pass.

SVSM went 27-0 season that year. James averaged 18 points, 6.2 rebounds, and 3.6 assists per game his freshman year, where they would go on to win the Division III state title.

Sophomore Year

SVSM repeated winning the state title that year under the leadership of James. They had a 26-1 record. James improved his numbers to a dominating 25.3 points, 7.4 rebounds and 5.5 assists per game. He showcased his dominance in a number of games where he scored 30 points or more 8 times during his sophomore season. He also had games dropping five or more assists 18 times. James' game was blossoming and it was around this time the media hype train would begin their religious visits to Akron.

Junior Year – Rise to Fame

As LeBron and his SVSM team were receiving unprecedented national coverage, there was a slight drop off in the team's production. While they still won 23 games and only lost 4 games, James and his team had an overwhelming amount of confidence. James began to be recognized as the Chosen One by Sports Illustrated, where he was the headlining cover athlete of that issue. With this exponential rise in fame, LeBron's basketball career took a dip. It was his junior year when he learned a humbling lesson that would set up a season for the ages the next year.

Games were played in nearby Akron University. The small high school gym SVSM had could not support the amount of people who wanted to come and see the mythical James play. Tickets were being sold for more than $100. Never had a high school athlete garnered so much attention. It began to get into LeBron's head, something he later acknowledged. The attention began to affect the team as well as they started to expect winning every game. The lack of humility was something they paid for in their bidding for the state title.

At the Division II Championship, SVSM fell to Roger Bacon (RB), a school they beat in the regular season. They walked into the game expecting to win their third straight state championship. Roger Bacon played a slow-paced, stalling style of basketball that frustrated SVSM. With no shot clock present in the high school system, RB played a patient game where they would swing the ball until they found an opening. By half time, SVSM finally woke up to reality and made an attempt to rally back. It wouldn't be enough. Roger Bacon also implemented a crafty strategy that is often seen in the NBA: let the superstar get his points, but do whatever you can do shut down the team. SVSM's lackadaisical habits and absence of preparation cost them the state title and James went home empty handed.

It was an extremely painful moment for the young team, who had not lost in such a stinging fashion in many years. It brought them to a similar time when the Fab 4 had missed out on winning an AAU title back in middle school. LeBron began considering heading into the 2002 NBA Draft as a seventeen-year-old. However, the NBA would not allow this, as they were firm on having their athletes graduate from high school.

A new resilient energy would be forged. LeBron, Sian, Dru, Willie and the rest of the SVSM crew would put in work that summer, in an attempt to earn the respect and humility they once carried.

Senior Year – Redemption

LeBron's senior year would be the year SVSM transcended the media attention, at least on the basketball end of things. With their loss from the last year, their focus was locked in on basketball. This is not to say the barrage of controversies and distractions stopped. There was an infamous Hummer incident that potentially could have derailed James' final year of high school. Gloria James was able to receive a loan to buy a Hummer for James' 18th birthday. However, this was a violation according to the Ohio High School Athletic Association. The rules stated that a high school player like James is in no position to receive gifts of $100 or more as a result of their athletic achievements. James would be banned from high school sports for the remainder of the season.

It was a difficult time for James, as SVSM was in the middle of a fantastic season. The new resilience forged the previous summer made them an unstoppable team, but a minor infraction of the rules potentially ruined their final year. James cried during the practices as he watched helplessly.

With no other options, James decided that appealing to the court would be his last hope. James, who was in a situation no other student has been in before, was forgiven by the OHSAA. The ban was reduced to a two game suspension. The athletic association acknowledged that this was an atypical situation and much blame could not be put on James. In his comeback, LeBron showed why he was the leader of the SVSM team by scoring a career-high of 52 points.

SVSM went 25-1 that year, with their only loss coming from a mandatory forfeit. James and his best friends were able to reach the goal they had set out to accomplish the previous summer by reclaiming the state title.

Work Ethic as a Student

LeBron, while not able to replicate his basketball wizardry on schoolwork, took pride in being a student. Amidst the plane trips to shoe companies, dealing with the press, and dominating the court, James still found a way to keep up with his schoolwork. Teachers were often impressed with his ability to hand in his assignments on time, despite his hectic schedule.

Middle school basketball coach and mentor, Frankie Walker, helped James' develop this work ethic. He, like many coaches who understood how to balance life, made sure LeBron made his classwork and chores a priority. LeBron would always have to help out around his temporary home and attend classes on a consistent basis in order to be able to play basketball. Walker was a great mentor in James' life.

Chapter 3: LeBron's NBA Career

The Draft

The 2003 NBA Draft class was rated one of the most talented draft classes in the history of the National Basketball Association. With the likes of Wade, Bosh, Carmelo and James, there has rarely been a time where so many franchise-altering players were in one draft. NBA writer Brian Windhorst made a key observation in his essay about the draft: the NBA was in the midst of a superstar decline. There were big shoes to be filled in the NBA. The 80s had Magic and Bird. The 90s had Michael Jordan alongside the likes of Charles Barkley, Patrick Ewing, Karl Malone, John Stockton and Hakeem Olajuwon. The 2000s started off shaky as the kind of talent that would elevate the NBA to international stardom began to fade. This is not to say there was a lack of talent from a pure basketball standpoint. There were players like Tracy McGrady, Tim Duncan, Vince Carter, and Kevin Garnett.

However, they weren't the international icons businesses could use to take their brand to the next level. As much as it may seem that the NBA is all about basketball, it is also a business competing with the likes of giant organizations operating their own sports leagues. Tennis had Andre Agassi. Soccer had the likes of David Beckham and Ronaldinho spearheading their sports. Tiger Woods was becoming the international star for golf. Besides the dominant Lakers squad, it was clear the NBA faced a superstar deficit, lacking in the kind of superstar brands that the NBA needed to grow overseas. This underscored the importance of the revolutionary draft that took place in this particular year. The 2003 NBA Draft was a huge victory for the league as a whole, as it would mark the revival of the new NBA fans see today. Jordan's retirement marked the end of the championship Bulls team loved by the world. It marked the end of the fierce rivalries between the Bulls and all the gutsy teams they faced: the notorious Detroit Pistons that made a name for themselves by locking down Jordan and the Knicks franchise led by Patrick Ewing. All the historic narratives seemed to come to a close, but it would be this monumental draft that would carry the torch passed by the previous decade.

As the season moved to full playoff mode, the bottom fourteen teams had all their hopes in getting that first pick. LeBron James was the clear first pick of the draft. He was on everyone's radar, including the lottery teams. If their projections were right, LeBron could turn around an entire franchise. The narrative was laid out for many teams. Cleveland, who tied for the league's worst record with the Nuggets at 17-65, would be bringing a homegrown talent into their organization. The Toronto Raptors could use LeBron to change the course of their losing ways. The Raptors were also in the middle of rebuilding after losing their franchise All-Star, Vince Carter. The Denver Nuggets were in the midst of a depression, similar to the

Cavaliers, after having multiple losing seasons for the past half-decade.

On May 22nd, 2003, the lottery that preceded the historic draft took place. It was here where the fates of numerous franchises would be sealed. The destiny of the NBA as a successful business entity would begin to unfold on this day as well. For LeBron, who was just weeks away from graduating from St. Vincent St. Mary's, the lottery was a suspenseful event. Just the day before, he had become one of the wealthiest eighteen-year-olds when he signed a deal with Nike that would eventually end up landing him over $100 million in earnings. And now all that was left was to find out which team he would play for.

As the lottery results were coming out, LeBron watched with friends and family at a ceremony titled the LeBron James Lottery Party. One by one the picks were coming out and LeBron pondered which team he would end up with. Could it be the Bulls? The Bulls were in the lottery picture, and having idolized Michael Jordan as a kid, it was likely LeBron played out fantasies of taking the Bulls back to their glory days. The Bulls were not that far behind the Cavs, as they had the 6th best odds (a 4.4% chance) in landing the coveted pick. Or would it be the historic franchise of the New York Knicks? The Knicks, although not possessing strong odds, were also in the lottery with a 1.5% chance to win it all. LeBron could see himself playing in the bright shining lights of Madison Square Garden. Being the face of one of the world's most internationally renowned cities never seems like a bad idea. Perhaps, LeBron could represent his home state of Ohio if Cleveland won the lottery. LeBron had strong ties with the state of Ohio from moving house-to-house, living without a father, to playing alongside the Fab 5 (the Fab 4 were renamed the Fab 5 after the addition of Romeo Travis) members and winning national titles. It was from these humble beginnings where James had developed strong roots for his city.

Because of the hometown connection, playing for Cleveland seemed just as good as playing for big cities like New York and Chicago.

As the fourth pick went to the Toronto Raptors, the top three teams in contention for James were Cleveland, Memphis and Denver. The Memphis Grizzlies were in a precarious position. Due to a prior trade with the Pistons, if the Grizzlies did not win the first pick, their pick would be automatically sent to the Pistons. Before the announcement of the top three picks, LeBron recalled in an interview saying he had a feeling he was going to stay in Ohio. After the commercial break, it was the Denver Nuggets who would receive the third pick, while the Memphis Grizzlies lost their pick by falling short as they received the second overall pick. LeBron's prediction before the commercial break was right. Cleveland had won the coveted 2003 Draft Lottery. At this time, moments before even the first pick was announced, LeBron's friends and family members were jumping on him. In storybook fashion, it would be the Cavaliers who would accommodate James. For a slight moment, LeBron finally had some peace and security. For James, he could close a chapter of his life and begin looking forward to a brand new life: a life away from poverty and a lack of security. He could look forward to a new life where he could work on becoming one of the greatest basketball players to have ever lived.

Coming off a poor 17-65 season, LeBron and his new Cavs team had plenty of ground to cover before they would become contenders. Before James' historic arrival, the future of the Cavaliers was bleak. Cumulatively over the past half-decade, the Cavs had a record of 130-248 (0.344 W/L Ratio). The losing culture permeated throughout the franchise. With James, the Cavaliers finally had new hope.

Rookie Season – Rookie of the Year

LeBron's rookie year was surrounded by heavy dosages of media attention. Everyone wanted to know how the boy out of Akron, Ohio could play in the big leagues. NBA veterans were excited to put LeBron in his place.

LeBron would establish himself the same way he did in high school, by dominating offensively with his athleticism and making his teammates better with his passing ability. Out of the gates, in a highly covered game against the Sacramento Kings, James scored 25 points, which set a record for most points for a player who came straight out of high school.

The overall team was not very good however. There were growing pains in the Cavaliers as they were turning around a franchise that was in the midst of a five-year slide. For the first five games, the Cavaliers went on a 5 game slide against tough teams like the Pacers who were one of the strongest teams at the time, led by Jermaine O'Neal and Reggie Miller. LeBron's Cavs went on another 8 game losing streak. Their record after their first 20 games was 5-15. In the midst of the losing, James was finding his groove. He averaged 16.5 points in those 20 games, which included a career high of 33 points, a record that would be quickly broken within a few weeks.

Things began to pick up for James. In the next 20 games, he elevated his team by averaging an impressive 24.4 points and 6 assists a game. The team managed to play a bit better, rising with an 8-12 record. The remaining 42 games, the Cavaliers played close to .500 basketball. Despite their 35-47 record, the second half of the season was a sneak preview in terms of how much James could affect the game. The impact was immediate as James changed the dynamic of a team that in its previous season had a 17-65 record. The growing pains were relatively short, compared to other franchises that go through years of development of their main star. On March 27, 2004, James went on a tear against talented New Jersey Nets team. He beat his previous career high of 38 points and went on to score 41 points.

With a rookie season for the ages, James snagged the NBA Rookie of the Year Award with ease. He won his award by being a valuable rookie chipping in 20.9 points, 5.5 boards and 5.9 assists on a nightly basis.

2004-05: James' Rise to the All-Star Level

James and his modified Cavaliers all of a sudden looked like dark horses in the East. In their first 20 games, James led his team to a 12-8 record. For 40 games, they maintained their winning percentage and were at 24-16. While not an elite team in the NBA, it came as a shock to many fans how quickly the Cavs seemed to be rebuilding. This was a testament to LeBron's talent, as he exploded into a basketball monster in his sophomore year. He averaged a stunning 25 points, 7.4 assists and 7.4 rebounds per game as a mere 19-year-old going on 20. Fans were witnessing a prodigy in the making, as LeBron immediately became one of the premier players of the league. Heading into the All-Star Break, LeBron was voted in as a starter for the Eastern Conference All-Star Team.

LeBron contributed 13 points, six assists and eight rebounds in a victory against the west. He joined the likes of Kobe and Magic Johnson when he became an All-Star by the time he was 20.

The rise to prominence took a minor bump as the surging Cavs team slowed down. James improved his averages in the remainder of the season, but his team played sub-par basketball, leading to a 42-40 record. The team did not participate in the 2005 NBA Playoffs. In the midst of their slip, the Cavaliers fired head coach Paul Silas for not keeping things together. Although the team lost its footing post-All-Star Weekend, they still had improved from their 35-47 record. This marked the second year straight of improvement in the James era.

2005-06: First Playoffs Appearance

LeBron James, already an All-Star, had done a steady job laying down the tracks of his legacy. The next mission was to take his team to the playoffs.

The Cavaliers hired Mike Brown, a defensively minded coach that was expected to take the Cavs to the next level. Their off-season player acquisition came in the form of Larry Hughes. Hughes was in the midst of playing in his prime and the Cavs saw him as a worthy investment for the 2005-2006 season.

The Cavaliers were back in early 2004-2005 form. Their record going into the All-Star game was 31-21, nearly identical to their record from the previous year. During this time, James seemed to crack through another ceiling, posting 31.2 points, 6.6 assists and seven rebounds per game. He was once again voted in as an All-Star.

In the 2006 NBA All-Star Game, James made his mark as a superstar. With the East behind by as much as 21 points an explosive LeBron scored 29 points and snatched six rebounds to regain control. James was awarded with the All-Star MVP, capping off an extremely successful weekend for James.

It was back to work for James and his Cavs. Knowing the downfall they experienced in the previous season after the All-Star break, the Cavs were weary of what could happen. Things looked like they would slip again, as they experienced a five-game losing streak, which included losses to potential playoff teams, the Wizards and the Pistons. The Cavs would stop the sliding and go on a 9 game winning streak a few weeks later.

The Cavaliers were back in the playoff scene after a long seven-year slump. It was James who spearheaded the change, where he averaged an incredible 31.4 points, 6.6 assists and 7 rebounds per game. James was awarded All-NBA First Team Honors for the first time, a list he would continue to make many times in the future. With the 50-32 record, the Cavs were in prime position to win in the first round.

In just his third year, James took his team to the playoffs. It was one of the faster turnarounds of a rebuilding franchise under the leadership of a franchise star. After just barely missing the playoffs the previous year, the Cavaliers improved to 50-32 this year. To go with his team's success, James was breaking records left and right, acquiring accolade after accolade, and was becoming an international icon for the NBA.

The Cavaliers would face a talented Wizards team. The Cavaliers had lost 1-3 in their season series. The Wizards were also in the midst of turning things around after their Jordan years. The Wizards had a trio of Antawn Jamison, Caron Butler and Gilbert Arenas. Arenas was one of the deadliest closers at the time.

James would play his heart out in the first game, putting up an amazing triple-double stat of 32-11-11. He led his team to a victory that night. The Wizards responded in the next game by forcing James to commit 10 turnovers. The Cavs and Wizards went toe-to-toe throughout the rest of the series. The two teams each split games on their home court. The next two games for the Cavaliers had extremely tight margins. Each game was decided by a victory of one point in overtime. It was James and his Cavaliers who came out the winners of the series.

James showed great poise in his first ever playoff series. In games that mattered, James showed that he could play. The criticism would not fall on him until his later years. James averaged 35.7 points, 5.7 assists and 7.5 rebounds in his first ever playoff round. There wouldn't be time to celebrate however, as the former Eastern Conference Playoff Champions were their next opponent.

The Detroit Pistons were hungry for a shot at the title, as they lost in their previous year in the Finals versus the Spurs. The Cavaliers led by a young James were now in their way to the title. Once again, James showed what he was capable of by averaging 26.6 points, 8.6 rebounds and 6 assists in a close seven game series. The series did go to 7 games but it had more to do with the Pistons not taking care of business. They were a team that was more than capable of taking care of a young LeBron and his Cavs squad. After winning the first two games, the Pistons got away from their defensive schemes. They dropped the next three games. However, the Pistons would awake from their slumber. The veteran line up of Rasheed Wallace, Chauncey Billups, Ben Wallace and Rip Hamilton knew how to turn it on when their backs were against the wall. The Pistons' defense stifled the rest of the Cavaliers team and took the series in 6. This included a complete shutdown where the Cavs were limited to 61 points in their Game 7 elimination match.

In spite of the playoff exit, all that mattered was that James' game was evolving every year. Their record always continued to improve, and in just his first year, they were able to take the previous Eastern Conference Champions to 7 games. It seemed like it would only be a matter of time before James would reach the peak.

2006-07: First Trip to the NBA Finals

This was the year LeBron showed fans why he was the self-proclaimed king. They repeated their 50-32 record, which did not reflect the improvement they made in years past, but James would again take his game to the next level in the playoffs. This season marked the beginning of James' championship aspirations. In the team huddles, they would have the ring and championship chants that contending teams used. The 2007 Playoffs featured LeBron's 48-point game as well as a visit to the Finals.

James was back in the playoffs, this time with his vision locked onto winning a ring for his city. The Cavaliers started off the playoffs by facing against a familiar foe. They were matched up against the Wizards, who were now considered their rivals.

However, James would not be caught up in the media narratives. The Cavs were simply the better team and the Wizards could not find an answer. The Cavaliers won the series against the Wizards with a 4-0 sweep. The next round was against a New Jersey Nets team, who had just won against their heated rivals, the Toronto Raptors. This team featured the trio of Vince Carter, Richard Jefferson and Jason Kidd. The series featured games that were tightly contested once again. The Nets trio was one of the most clutch trios in the NBA, hitting daggers in the fourth, but they wouldn't be given such an opportunity, as the Cavs would play impressive fourth quarters throughout the series. The Cavs won in six, and for the first time in James' career, he was headed to the Eastern Conference Finals.

The Eastern Conference Finals featured another rematch against the Pistons. At the time, the Pistons were considered the better team. Experts had predicted that the Pistons would square off in a rematch against the Spurs, but it was James' clutch play that changed the destiny of the potential rematch. Initially, the Pistons took care of home court advantage in typical fashion, just as they did in the year before. However, there was a déjà-vu moment as the Cavs won the next two games. With the series tied at 2-2 again, James set his mark; ensuring things would be different this year. In a historic Game 5 against the Pistons, LeBron went on one of the most impressive scoring streaks in NBA history. He led his team to a victory in double OT. James notably scored 29 of the remaining 30 Cavalier points. Leading 3-2, exactly like in the previous year, the coaching staff made a point about how dangerous the Pistons could be. They headed into the game with full awareness of what could happen, and closed the Pistons out in the 6th game. It was an unexpected victory compared to what the experts had predicted. In his young career, James was already headed to the NBA Finals.

It was a story for the ages: from poverty in Akron to being a high school phenomenon to an NBA Finals participant, all in such a short span of time. Perhaps it came a bit too fast. James would not make the NBA Finals again until he began playing for the Miami Heat. To fulfill his role as the Chosen One, James had an enormous obstacle to pass. It was the first time the Cavs played against a well-established Spurs team, whose core had won multiple championships. Experts had the Spurs winning anywhere from five to seven games. James and his Cavaliers would need to dig deep to win against a veteran championship team.

The Spurs defensive game plan was to shut down James. Bruce Bowen, one of the elite defenders at the time, contained James to a poor Finals start. As a result, the Cavaliers had to hustle to catch up against the steady Spurs. Unable to rally, James had his first experience of what Finals-quality defense looked like. Down 0-1, the Cavs tried to make adjustments to move the ball around more.

The adjustments would be in vain as the Spurs Big 3 of Parker, Ginobili and Duncan came to take care of business in San Antonio. They combined for a total of 78 points, with Parker leading the way with his 30. The Spurs offense was flawless and it almost looked like they were on their way to a sweep. Although James scored 25 points, it was a far cry from his previous playoff performances where he would dominate games.

Back in Cleveland, the Cavaliers looked to protect their home court. However, the experience of the Spurs proved to be too much for the Cavs. In every situation, the Spurs knew how to respond. Whether the Cavs would go on a mini run, or James would show flashes of brilliance, it was Coach Pop and his team who knew how to effectively respond. The Spurs took care of the Cavs on their home floor and won the 2007 NBA Finals in four games.

This marked the beginning of James' tough and excruciating journey in competing for the championship. With a taste of what the finals were like, James would train hard in the off-season to prevent embarrassing himself in the Finals the next year.

2007-08: Struggles against the Celtics

The Eastern Conference Champions strangely didn't add much to their line-up. Their core of Ilgauskas, Hughes, Gooden and James was largely untouched. This was not a good sign for a team that needed lots of improvement to fend off a team like the Spurs.

The lack of improvement showed. This was the year the Celtics assembled the Big 3, and the Western Conference teams were rising. Every team from the first seed to the eighth seed in the West was competitive. The Cavs weren't in that conference, but they needed to improve nevertheless to keep up with the competition. It seemed like the Cavs were the same team from last year. After not being able to keep up their improvement from the previous season, they made a mid-season trade to revamp their core. They traded away Drew Gooden and Larry Hughes for Ben Wallace and Delonte West. They also acquired Wally Szczerbiak, who was a shooting guard that added depth in the two spot for the Cavs.

As a big chunk of their team was shifted, the Cavs had a difficult time gaining traction and ended up with a 45-37 record. The assembly of the Big 3 in Boston had paid off. Behind their 66-16 record, the Celtics looked like contenders and the Cavs looked like they had to play from behind.

The Cavaliers faced off against their playoff rivals, the Washington Wizards. The rivalry hit its peak as shots were fired on the court and off the court. Deshawn Stevenson notably told the media that James was overrated. LeBron fired back with 32 points, taking Game 1. James and his Cavaliers performed masterfully in Game 2 against their rivals, leading to a blowout win of 116-86. Washington would take one win at home with a blowout, but the Cavaliers stole a Game 4, leading 3-1. This year's Wizards wouldn't back down, as they won a game on the Cavaliers home floor in an elimination game. In the sixth game, the Cavaliers proved they were the kings of the rivalry with a commanding 105-88 victory. They would wait for the Celtics, who were in the midst of a heated seven game series with Atlanta Hawks.

The Celtics faced a new challenge in the Cleveland Cavaliers. Despite the Cavs' less than stellar show in the regular season, they looked like a team that had composure in their previous round against the Wizards. Ben Wallace and their new point guard Delonte West seemed to be comfortable playing with James.

This series came down to the team that possessed home court advantage. It was a dogfight between the two teams, as each team took turns winning every time they were on their home floor. The Celtics started 2-0 while they shut down James. James would continue his poor shooting in Cleveland, but was able to win through finding his teammates. The series eventually tied up at 3-3, went back to Boston for one final game. James faced elimination, after having just made the finals. His reputation was on the line, and he played fiercely. James scored 45, but Celtics were able to edge out the Cavs with a 97-92 victory. The Celtics were the eventual NBA champs. James and the Cavs had some thinking to do over the off-season.

Olympic Summer Redeem Team

James went on to play in Beijing's 2008 Summer Olympics. The USA Basketball program was in the midst of trying to re-establish the dominance they once had. After a poor showing in the 2004 Olympics, Team USA needed to revamp their basketball program and demand greatness. The team featured some of the greatest players of the 2000's era. The team featured Kobe Bryant, Dwyane Wade, Dwight Howard, Chris Paul and LeBron James.

With their pride on the line, 2008 Team USA squad displayed dominance on the global stage.

James was a tremendous contributor as he did his fair share in scoring and also facilitating Team USA Coach Krzyzewski's offense. James averaged 15.5 points, 3.8 assists and 5.2 rebounds in his Olympic appearance.

They would be eventual gold medalists, beating Spain in a close game, until Kobe Bryant took over in the fourth quarter with his 'Black Mamba' persona.

James learned a tremendous amount from this team. He saw how guys like Bryant and Wade prepared for games, which served as a valuable learning experience. It also served as a glimpse into the Miami Big 3 that made shock waves across the basketball world.

2008-09: A Repeat Eastern Conference Playoff Exit

Having played with the world's best team, this time around, LeBron seemed prepared to take his team to the next level. Last year, they had other excuses. They were trying to integrate freshly acquired Ben Wallace and Delonte West in the middle of the season, and had no real point guard. The 2008 Cavaliers had no identity in their point guard position. They had a collection of guards who weren't true point guards in essence. Daniel Gibson, Delonte West and Damon Jones could've all been labeled as the "guard" type point guard. This is the type of point guard that is better at contributing as a shooter, but too small to be playing the shooting guard. To address their issues, they brought in Maurice Williams. After losing to the Celtics, the Cavaliers seemed like they had learned their lesson. They were on top of the Eastern Conference column with a franchise record breaking

66-16. James was also awarded the NBA MVP Award for helping take his team to the upper echelon.

The Cavaliers looked to be the favorite to contend against the Lakers. With their dominating sweeps against Detroit and Atlanta, the Cavaliers were waiting in anticipation for their next target. While the Cavaliers were resting their legs, the Orlando Magic and the Celtics were in the midst of a series that eventually would go to seven games. The stars were lined up for James and his Cavaliers. Orlando came out as the eventual winners against the Celtics. A fast paced team awaited the Cavaliers.

The Magic beat the Cavs in their season series 2-1. There were match-up issues for the Cavaliers during that regular season. Orlando's sharpshooting front and backcourt caused many problems for the Cavs, just as they did for many teams in the NBA that season. The Cavaliers and their fans would forget the past. There have been times where a team would lose the season series, but show up as a different beast in the playoffs. The Cavaliers could say they were well rested, while the Magic were fatigued coming out of an intense series. Besides LeBron, the fast paced, inside-out gameplay of the Orlando Magic seemed to punish a Cavaliers team that played at a slower tempo. Bigs like Varejao and Ilgauskas were no match for the extremely mobile front court the Magic had. In previous outings, the Magic won with a holistic approach, playing basketball where everyone got touches and had opportunities to score. They ran an offense with an emphasis on playing a crafty inside-out style created by Stan Van Gundy. Dwight would play like the superstar center he was known to be, dominating the post, which attracted attention, leaving deadly shooters like Courtney Lee, Rashard Lewis, Hedo Turkoglu and J.J. Redick open on the floor. The Cavaliers would have matched up better against the Celtics, especially with Garnett down and out for the season. The one thing the Cavs had going for them was the momentum they had from crushing teams in the previous rounds. With 4-0 sweeps against both Detroit and Atlanta, there was a sense of confidence going into the Eastern Conference Finals. They were the owners of a 66-16 record, with a renewed scent of blood in their playoff appearances.

Game 1 was a heated battle and LeBron showed up to claim what he and his team wanted. He would end up scoring 49 points on an efficient 20 for 30 shooting, while dishing out the ball eight times and grabbing six boards to round out his stats. Things were clicking for the Cavs. They also had a bit of a lucky stroke. Mo Williams would hit a ¾ court shot at the half time buzzer to put his team up 63-48. They played good team basketball, racking up 23 assists and having only five turnovers. By the half, with the type of basketball they were playing, it looked like James was ready to go back into the finals. Two sweeps and Game 1 with a 15 point lead going to the half? Bring on the NBA Finals.

Bit by bit, Howard and his Magic had different ideas. Rashard Lewis was on fire in the second half raining three's from outer space, and Turkoglu was orchestrating the brilliant offense set up by Van Gundy. It appeared that the Magic were burnt out from their seven game series against Boston, but they were right back in form as they were playing the fluid basketball they were known for. They trailed by as much as 16 points, but it was the efficient gameplay of the Magic that would put them in a position ready to edge out the Cavaliers just when it mattered. In the last minute, Rashard Lewis hit a three to put up the Magic by one. James and the Cavaliers ended up losing their first game in the 2009 NBA Playoffs. The sky high Cavaliers fell back down to Earth. James played an amazing game, but it was the three-point bomb-dropping Magic that proved to be an alarming threat to James' hopes for a title.

It was Game 2 and the Cavs needed to win this game. The Cavaliers led as much as by 23 points in this game, but the Magic had been in a similar situation before. They knew their efficient three-point shooting could quietly bring them back. In the critical moments of the game, with around 30 seconds left, the game was tied, and the ball was in LeBron's hands. He drove to the basket and seemed to pick up the ball too early. He was called for a travel. Hedo Turkoglu would score on the next possession and put his Magic up 95-93 with a second left in regulation.

Out of the time-out, James hit a game winning three-pointer that would save the Cavaliers from being in a 0-2 hole.

The situation was worrying for the Cavaliers at this point. James did score one of the biggest baskets of his life up to that point, but the Magic gave them a tough time on their own home court. With the exception of the final shot, Orlando had the team that seemed to be fairly in control. James' fairy-tale shot only seemed to mask their deficiencies. The Cavs barely tied it up at home. What would it be like playing on the road? The Magic had an answer for that.

The Magic played as if the shot didn't happen. They cleaned up the Cavs when the series went over to Orlando. The Magic was able to come away with two wins on their home court. LeBron's 41 and 44-point finishes on the road were simply not enough. This brought the Magic to a convincing 3-1 lead. Basketball experts could not have foreseen the hole the Cavaliers put themselves in. Many experts had the Cavaliers winning the series in anywhere from five to seven games.

In a desperate Game 5, LeBron played one of the best games of his career. Putting up 37 points, 12 assists, and 14 rebounds, James led his Cavaliers to a 112-102 victory. The Magic, however, played an uncharacteristic game, hitting only 32% of their three-pointers. Their fluid basketball game was non-existent, as they finished with 12 assists and 12 turnovers.

Despite these stats, the Magic was still able to put up a good fight. If the Magic went on one of their hot streaks, it would spell the end of the Cavaliers season.

Game 6 would be played in Orlando. The Magic was able to fully utilize the support from their fans in their last game at home. The Orlando Magic went back to their inside out game, dropping three-pointers after three-pointers. They hit an efficient 12-29 from downtown, and a surprising 17-21 from the free throw line. Despite being one of the league's worst free throw shooting teams at the time due to Howard's inconsistent performance; they were able to hit 81% that night, with Howard hitting 12 for 16. In addition to his great performance from the line, Howard racked up an incredible 40 points and 14 rebounds.

James played in what was one of the best series in his playoff career. With numerous 40-point appearances, and the buzzer-beating shot, it further cemented his greatness. However, these kinds of feats were an expectation from James. People knew he could dominate games. Now, fans wanted to see a champion. But he would be thwarted again, this time by the rising Magic squad led by a core of Howard, Lewis and Turkoglu.

This was the year the comparisons and the criticisms began to rain over LeBron. LeBron was now a max contract player with max contract expectations. It was just two seasons ago that LeBron stood head-to-head against the mighty Spurs in the finals. Even though the Cavs posted the best season Cleveland has ever witnessed, it seemed odd that they were not participating in the 2009 Finals against the great Lakers team led by Bryant and Gasol. Early playoff exits to the Celtics and Magic seemed to derail James' godlike legacy during these years.

2009-10: Struggle against the Celtics Part II & James' Disappearing Act

The 2009-2010 NBA season was a big year for James, the Cavs and the NBA. The big free agent bonanza was coming up. Teams were frantically trying to cater to their superstars so they could win a title. The Raptors acquired Hedo Turkoglu to take Bosh and the rest of the team to the next level. It seemed like members of the Cavs front office were doing a decent job adding in new talent every year to complement LeBron's all-around game. First it was the acquisition of a gritty Ben Wallace to boost their defensive efforts. Then in the beginning of the '09 season, they got a point guard in Mo Williams, who seemed to be heading into the prime of his career. After losing to the Orlando Magic squad and its extremely fluid front court and amazing shooters the Cavaliers tried to address the speed the team was lacking. They added three-point sharpshooter Anthony Parker and snagged Antawn Jamison who would play the four for them.

On paper, this looked like it would address all the issues they faced against the Magic.

Fans often forget that the Cavs did in fact try to support James with the right pieces. The Cavs franchise was heavily scrutinized after the season for not bringing in enough talent for James. Although James was not paired with a superstar player, there were many smart veterans on the team. The Cavs had the kinds of veterans a contending team would have—ones who could refine a decent team into a great one. Jamison was a key piece in the Wizards' rise a few years back. Anthony Parker was a seasoned veteran, having played in the Euroleague, and having served as a consistent three-point shooter for the Toronto Raptors. Along with adding mobility to their team, they needed a rim protector to play against Dwight Howard. To match their dominant big man, the Cavs recruited their own superman, Shaquille O'Neal. In the media day of Shaq's signing, he famously said that he would "win a ring for the king." It seemed like the

Cavs were poised to win with all these acquisitions. The last year against the Magic was just a minor blip in the radar. Now they truly had everything they needed to overcome any adversity. They too had sharpshooters in Williams, Anthony Parker and a four who could stretch the floor in Antawn Jamison. They too had a roster that could match the more mobile teams in the NBA, like the Magic.

The Cavaliers maintained dominance with a 61-21 Record, winning the race in the Eastern Conference. Unfortunately, for a third year straight, The Cavaliers would fall victim to a team that would go on to participate in the NBA Finals.

The seasoned Celtics, whose main core had now played for three years, were in redemption mode as well, coming off an Eastern Conference Semifinal exit. What added more complexity to their redemption process was that Garnett was lost in the process due to a season ending injury. If their chances for a repeat were thrown off merely because of a missing vital piece, they knew they would be the team to be heading into the Finals if they could just stay healthy. It was just last year where the Celtics took the Magic to seven games without Garnett. The "what if's" lingered in the minds of the Celtics organization. Along with that, the team's core was aging, and they didn't know when they would be playing their last games together. Here was a team with a sense of purpose. And this did not bode well for James.

Once again, the Cavaliers got off to a good start in the 2010 NBA Playoffs. Matched up against the eighth seeded Chicago Bulls, the Cavaliers' experience would give them a triumphant 4-1 series victory. Their upcoming foes also finished in similar fashion. The Celtics were in a battle against Dwyane Wade and the Miami Heat. The Celtics won the series 4-1 with their own core of Allen, Rondo, Garnett and Pierce taking turns disassembling a Miami Heat team that lacked depth.

It was a rematch against the Celtics, who were hungry to win a title after getting back a healthy Kevin Garnett. The Celtics were a tremendous foe. They nearly stole two games on the road, as they took Game 2 in an 18-point victory on the Cavs home court. The Cavs retaliated when they arrived in Boston with a blowout Game 3 victory of 124-95, while James scored a ferocious 38 points. The Celtics remained composed and were able to knot up the series at 2-2. The Celtics would surprise the Cavs with a stifling second half in front of the Cavaliers' crowd in Game 5. It was another blowout victory, but this time for the Celtics, who won 120-88. Game 6 was an exciting affair to watch. The teams went back and forth until the Celtics started pulling away in the third quarter. Ray Allen and Pierce took turns landing three's in the gut of the Cavaliers' defense. The Cavs would make a final run in the fourth, but ultimately fall short. With James' back against the wall, he was unable to deliver in Game 6. He was able to rack up an impressive 27 points, 19 rebounds, and 10 assists triple double, but it meant nothing when they lost their shot at the title. The Cavaliers season came to a shocking end. They were unable to take on an aging Celtics team; with a roster they thought would be enough to beat any team in the league. James' disappearance in his last game as a Cavalier was met by a torrential wave of criticism. Media analysts constantly projected the idea that James couldn't finish for the Cavs when it mattered most. It was a catchy headline that would be used to belittle James in the lengthy comparisons to previous stars.

Being touted as the "Chosen One", LeBron once again came under enormous scrutiny. He was not able to take his team past the Eastern Conference Semifinals, even with a revamped lineup. Their strong play in the regular season had no bearing in the playoffs. His team had played poorly in the playoffs and disappointed many NBA experts who had high expectations for the Cavaliers that year.

Chapter 4: LeBron's NBA Career – The Decision

LeBron had a new choice to make. As a father looking out for his family, and as a man chasing down a legacy, there were serious questions to be asked. In what city could he have the best opportunity to raise his kids? Which organization offered the best chance of winning a title? Did he need a fresh start somewhere else? How could his Cavaliers team, which seemed to add the right pieces, just never get over the hump in the playoffs? James had taken his Cavs and set franchise records for wins in the regular season. Could the Cavs add just one more piece? Was adding one more piece enough, or would it result in the Cavaliers being a great regular season team that exited before the Finals? On top of that, the constant criticism of not being a closer of games lingered over James. Being written off as someone who didn't have the intangible factors to win was a nagging issue. Despite these criticisms, LeBron was still touted as the best player in the game, and that meant he had options.

Heading into free agency, LeBron had various options to take his game to the next level. Teams were ready to give LeBron the pitch of the century. The Knicks, Nets, Clippers, Chicago, Miami and his Cavaliers were in the running for James. Each team offered dreamy futures. The Knicks, who had recently signed A'mare Stoudemire, could have a big two playing in The Big Apple. The Knicks had been building up exclusively for this summer and could offer big money for LeBron James. The Nets were in the process of moving to Brooklyn, and James could be the man leading the franchise toward a new destination. The business opportunities in Brooklyn may have been just as enticing as the ones presented by the Knicks. Chicago had a young core of Derrick Rose, Deng, and Joakim Noah. They were a team rising after years of missing the playoffs following Jordan's retirement. The Chicago Bulls had a new layer of tradition and culture that LeBron could be a part of. The Clippers were the only Western Conference team in the mix that offered something similar to what the Knicks could offer, which was their basketball culture. LeBron could help steer the losing ways of the Clippers and turn them into a powerhouse. While the Miami Heat could not offer the same kind of historicity that aged franchises like the Knicks had, the Heat had competent people running the organization. The emphasis of LeBron's visit was playing under championship mindsets. With Pat Riley running the office, LeBron would have a world-class legend to learn from. Despite facing challenges in the playoffs in recent years, Wade had won a championship with his amazing ability to score baskets in the past. LeBron could walk the beaten path and learn from A to Z what it took to become a champion. Chris Bosh joining the Heat in the midst of the entire 2010 free agency hurricane swayed LeBron as well. The Cavaliers did whatever they could to promise signing a marquee free agent. However, the city was not an enticing destination for free agents like Bosh. The Cavaliers' hopes for retaining James seemed slim.

It was reported that James did want to stay in Cleveland. He made attempts to attract Chris Bosh to Cleveland, but Bosh blitzed straight toward the sunny city of Miami after hearing what they had to offer. For LeBron, joining Bosh and going to the Miami Heat seemed to make the most sense. LeBron could round out the pair to create one of the most devastating trios of sports history.

What the other organizations couldn't offer to LeBron was a player who could teach LeBron what it took to win. After multiple playoff exits, LeBron was left humbled. He was dumbfounded, unable to make it to the top year after year. Dwyane Wade, a one-time champion, could show him the ropes. The Knicks and Nets had no such players. Neither did the Chicago Bulls. The other teams could only simply promise money and more money to throw at other free agents. The Miami Heat offered the exact same thing since they had cap space just like everyone else, but with added benefits. Unlike other franchises, the Heat had a contemporary champion in Dwyane Wade. One could argue the Cavs had Shaq, a champion in his own right, but Shaq was in the twilight of his career. The winning mentality Pat Riley commanded from the top seemed to be a key component as well. These were the intangible characteristics LeBron had to be sensitive enough to sense. He knew from past years, it wasn't enough to get good players on a team. He had the 60+ winning seasons. He had the MVPs. He had the team that would make necessary additions. But one thing he had yet to experience was being under the tutelage of a champion.

Perhaps due to him being constantly in the spotlight, LeBron missed the opportunity to learn under a great mentor. Dwyane Wade had Pat Riley and professional veterans like Alonzo Mourning to study the game with.

Kobe had Phil Jackson and a prime Shaq to learn from, and spent many years closely studying Jordan's game in his own time. The Spurs who won multiple titles had Greg Popovich, one of the greatest coaches in NBA history. Even Jordan, who seemingly did it all by himself had incredible mentors in Tex Winter and Phil Jackson, managing the superstar persona. Throughout his NBA career, James was always the leader, but how could he lead when he hadn't been a student of championship basketball? He was a great student of the game, but this was one of those hidden x-factors that LeBron needed to cover to transcend from just being a great regular season team. LeBron could learn under Wade, play under the watchful eye of Pat Riley and Erik Spoelstra, and work on his growth towards becoming a champion. Despite his move being perceived as cheap, weak-minded and unfair by fans and critics all over the world, it was a step that showed the humility of James, the kind of humility that a champion must embrace before becoming a champion.

He could have said he would do it himself, like fans wanted to see. It wasn't about that anymore at this critical point. What if James' knees wore out? What if he suffered from a devastating injury? James needed some kind of stability, and Miami seemed like it could provide it. His move to Miami was a move that symbolically paid respect to the process of becoming an all-time great.

The backlash was immense. The decision set in motion a chain of events that would eventually end up portraying LeBron James as the NBA's new villain. James was one of the most liked athletes internationally, but quickly turned into the most hated player overnight. The media judged James when he set up the decision without having the courtesy to tell the Cavaliers about his future moves. Having spent seven years with an organization, critics thought it only made sense to tell your work place where you're going. Added on to the lack of professionalism, fans didn't like the idea of superstars collaborating. Majority owner Dan Gilbert wrote a letter aggressively slandering James, calling him a traitor. He famously declared that the Cavs would also win a ring before James would.

The Heat was fortunate enough to have all three of their superstar players opt in for less money. This gave them the opportunity to bring in veterans like Mike Miller and resign veteran Udonis Haslem. The signing of these key pieces made the Miami Heat favorites to win the Eastern Conference.

2010-11: Villain Debut

LeBron James was a marked man coming into the 2010-2011 season. The antagonist narrative the Heat pinned on him was a headline that resonated throughout the basketball world. Even LeBron took on the role and embraced his new persona, a decision he would come to regret in the next year. The crimson colors of the Miami Heat added to the effect. The public viewed LeBron's arrival in Miami as a shallow move in an attempt to cut out the working process of building a contending team. Many argued that championship teams were won through internally developing the organization over many years. This new way of mechanically building a superstar team was a no-go for many basketball fans, as teams with development, culture and history were favored. The world had yet to see someone like Magic Johnson leave the showtime Lakers. Jordan stayed with the Bulls and revolutionized the city by building a dynasty over many years. Kobe endured growing pains together with the Lakers franchise as he faced heavy media criticism, but never left. It almost seemed like LeBron paved the path for superstars leaving their franchises. 2003 NBA Draft classmate Carmelo Anthony would leave his Nuggets in similar fashion, joining A'mare Stoudemire and the New York Knicks. Dwight Howard would also be a superstar whose popular and well-liked image fell when he left the

Orlando Magic to be part of a Lakers team featuring Kobe, Gasol and Nash.

In addition, the Big 3 held their welcoming event where James announced the Heat winning multiple rings. It was a gesture that added more passionate hate toward James. An immature move, which seemed to counterbalance the humble side he showed on multiple occasions throughout his storied career. As a human being, these were all learning experiences for James. No human is perfect, and James, having lived a life of extreme highs and lows, would be the first one to say this. His roller coaster life was in the public for everyone to see. These tough experiences would forge the LeBron we see today.

All throughout the season, LeBron played the bad guy. Boos rained on the Heat in nearly every road game they played. Everywhere James went he was the villain. Playing as a member of the Miami Heat was one of the most challenging times that James experienced.

Adding to the intense criticism, the Miami Heat got off to a slow start. A loss to Dallas set their record at 9-8. The 9-8 start was one of the biggest headlines in the sports world. The Miami Heat team, featuring Olympians Bosh, James, and Wade, did not appear to be gelling. Haters basked in the glow as they took this as proof of their theories that karma was not going James' way. Writers would once again come up with detailed predictions of how everything could fall apart. A minor physical bump between James and Spoelstra was under the microscope. Every critic gravitated toward this situation, while calling out the downward spiral they wanted to see. The Heat were truly the villains. Everybody outside of Miami wanted to see them lose.

In the midst of the fire, the Miami Heat held a crucial players-only meeting. At this meeting, a new mentality was in the process of being forged, as the members of the Heat refocused their vision solely on winning basketball games.

The meeting served of vital importance as the Heat turned things around winning 21 of their next 22 games. It would be a close game with Dallas that marred their chance of having won 22 straight. During the winning streak, LeBron played with ferocity. 12 out of the 22 times, LeBron lead his team in scoring, and putting up numerous 30+-point games. That December was the best month of the season. It was at one of the highest moments of scrutiny that James and his new team found a way to forge team chemistry under such high pressure. Coach Spoelstra won Coach of the Month honors, and James and Wade were co-recipients of Player of the Month.

By the time All-Star Weekend rolled around, James and Wade were voted to be All-Star starters. Chris Bosh was included in the mix as a reserve. It was a historic moment for the Miami Heat as it was the first time they were able to send three of their players to the famed event.

As the year came to a close, the decision James made proved to be the right one. The Heat were ranked second in the East with a 58-24 win-loss record, just behind the Chicago Bulls. LeBron's stats took a minor dip, averaging 26.7 points on an efficient 51% shooting percentage, combined with 7.5 and 7.0 rebounds and assists, respectively.

The 2011 NBA Playoffs were a hostile setting for the Heat. Their success on the court brought them to where they were expected to play, but at every level, from the beginning of the season, until the end, fans wanted to see the Heat endure a painful downfall. The Heat managed to carry out their hopes of winning by defeating a young and inexperienced Sixers team in the first round in five games. The Heat would then face the Boston Celtics. The Celtics were a team that had history of battling James and Wade on separate occasions. The Celtics sent James and his Cavaliers home on multiple occasions, and in the past year, they sent Wade's Heat out of the playoffs in five games. James and Wade showcased exciting basketball. The Celtics were facing a revolving door of superstars. One night it was James. Another night would be Wade and his smooth finishes to the rim. The old Celtics core was no match for the newly assembled Big 3.

The newly crowned MVP Derrick Rose and his Bulls were up next. However, the Heat never skipped a beat. Their Big 3 overpowered the defensively minded Bulls. This time it was one-two punch of Bosh and James that would take them on their first visit to the Finals as a Miami Heat team. It was James' second time in the Finals, since his last appearance in 2007 against the Spurs.

This year's opponent was a Dallas Mavericks team that seemed to know how to surgically take teams apart. It was this team that tore apart the previous year's championship Lakers team. Rick Carlisle and his coaching staff developed one of the best defenses in the NBA that year. They also beat the Heat in the regular season in their two meetings against each other. The first four games showed that it could've been anyone's title. However, the Mavericks had figured it out. They knew what it took to get the ball stuck in LeBron's hands. The Heat lacked movement and it looked as if James was set up in isolated situations too many times. There was no motion or fluidity in the Heat offense. Chandler manned the paint, Terry rained three's, and Nowitzki fired off his patented one-legged fade-aways to a 4-2 series victory.

2011-12: Championship

Despite making it all the way to the NBA Finals in the previous year, the situation in Miami did not look good. Erik Spoelstra was constantly in the media spotlight. Fans and analysts were questioning the chemistry between The Big 3. People were wondering when Pat Riley would fire Spoelstra and finally step down to lead The Big 3. As for LeBron, all fingers were pointed toward him, as the "LeChoke" and "LeBrick" monikers became popular with his detractors and haters. As of the end of the 2010-11 season, LeBron was still viewed as that really good player who couldn't finish when it mattered. Comparisons to the likes of Kobe and Jordan were sky high. He could not get rid of the ridicule that followed him throughout his years in Cleveland due to his inability to come out victorious under high-pressure situations. And lastly, he still had no ring after promising multiple titles in his infamous ceremony the summer before. The mentality was title or bust. With no title, it did not matter whether they made the NBA Finals. Titles were paramount in the Big 3 era.

This particular off-season was a critical point in LeBron's life. Having coming off an embarrassing loss to the Mavericks, LeBron would undergo a very contemplative time in his life. For two weeks, LeBron did not leave his house, speculating what went wrong with the 2010-2011 Miami Heat. He joined Dwyane Wade and Chris Bosh in what he thought was a world-class organization run by the likes of Pat Riley. Was the team dynamic off? Whose team was it? Was it Dwyane's or LeBron's, or was it shared? LeBron had to dig even deeper and truly acknowledge the difficulty of the path of winning a title. Even though he lined up the stars as much as he could, things still weren't exactly the way he had hoped. It was at this moment of reflection and introspection that Dwyane Wade would call him and invite him to the Bahamas. The two leaders of the Miami Heat would brainstorm for a solution that could potentially take them to the next level.

It was at that moment that Dwyane Wade offered LeBron more of an active leadership role. It was already formally established that Wade, Bosh and James were the leaders of the team. But what Wade was trying to convey was a message from somewhere deeper in his soul. He wanted LeBron to be the unquestioned leader that he was for the Cavaliers, now for the Heat. With his mind reset, LeBron refilled his glass with a new vision of where to take the team, while pouring out the remnants of the bad guy persona he portrayed the previous season. Wade was right. He knew he had to get back to being the leader he was in Cleveland. He had to get back to being the person who fell in love with the game of basketball.

With a newly clear-minded LeBron, the Heat would reset their sights on winning an NBA championship. The Heat was the favorite once again to make it to the NBA Finals. They also made some moves to solidify their chances of winning the title. The key acquisition of this summer was adding Shane Battier to the cast. Battier was a critical piece as he brought in many of the intangible factors championship teams tend to look for. Battier was known to be a great locker room presence in his prior teams with the Grizzlies and the

Rockets. Besides that, he has a high basketball IQ, operating efficiently and effectively on both sides of the court. He also helped spread the floor, joining Mike Miller with his ability to shoot the three.

The start of the 2011-2012 season was postponed by the NBA lockout. With the player union and the league unable to come to an agreement, NBA games were at a standstill until the Union finally relented to the aggressive demands by league executives. The shortened lockout season would start on Christmas Day.

The NBA would pair up the Mavericks and the Heat for a rematch of the previous year's NBA Finals. The Heat won that game and went on to win many more games that season. The Heat achieved a remarkable 46-20 season, just slightly under their previous mark of 58-24, which translated into a better win ratio, percentage-wise.

Entering the playoffs, the Miami Heat was in redemption mode. After all the talk of winning titles, they learned through their previous loss to the Mavericks that getting to the finals was no walk in the park, and this year would be no different.

This time around, they played against a New York Knicks team in the first round, a rising Indiana Pacer's squad in the Eastern Conference Semifinals, and then went seven games against the Celtics in the Conference Finals. James and his Heat would keep their eye on the prize. They constantly reminded themselves that they had been here before. They knew how to dig themselves out of deep situations now. Through the ups and downs, they were back in the NBA Finals, this time against a youthful Oklahoma City Thunder. It would be a star-studded event with Durant, Westbrook and James Harden battling against the returning Heat for the title.

Heading into this year's Finals, it looked like anybody could win the title. The season series was tied up at 1-1, and basketball experts could not agree on who would be the eventual champions. In Game 1, it would be the running, gunning and hustling style of OKC that would beat the Heat. The Thunder out-muscled the Heat on the glass and lead in fast break points, 24-4. Durant had a Jordan-esque stat line in his first ever appearance in the Finals with 36 points, four assists and eight rebounds, winning in his first duel against LeBron. With home court going for the Thunder, it looked like the Heat were the underdogs all of a sudden.

Then, the gears started to spin for Miami. Was it James' pain from all those years of not being able to win? It may have been the Finals from the previous year that galvanized the Heat. Bosh was in tears after their loss to Dallas, and James, who played poorly, was under heavy fire from the media once again. They stole a game on the Thunder's home floor by playing a solid three quarters, and preventing an intense comeback attempt. The Heat were conscious of how they lost their first game and limited fast-break scoring opportunities.

Game 3 was a gritty, low scoring match for teams who typically scored over 100 points per game. James, haunted by his poor showing in the previous Finals, played another great game with 29 points and 14 rebounds.

In the next game, they needed another hall of fame type showing from the King, which he delivered. A tired and burnt-out-looking James was able to contribute with 26 points, 12 assists and nine rebounds. James could barely stand after the game, but this was all part of the Finals experience. Nothing was more painful than his two previous Finals exits. In an extremely close Game 4, James came out with clutch baskets by hitting a tie-breaking three-point shot, after having suffered from painful leg cramps. They narrowly came out with the victory. James was able to lead his team to a 3-1 advantage.

One last home game in the 2-3-2 Finals schedule would be all that the Heat needed. James played consistently from Games 1 to 4 and would continue his relentlessness into the fifth and final game with an impressive triple-double performance of 26 points, 13 assists and 11 rebounds. The Heat held a commanding 15-point advantage over the Thunder going into the fourth and would extend it past the 20-point mark in the fourth quarter. The Thunder would try to rally back, but the lead was insurmountable. As the clock was winding down, all that was left was for the confetti to rain onto the court.

James won the title this year, receiving Finals MVP Honors for the first time in his career. It was an extremely difficult journey for James. At various times throughout his career, it seemed like he was never going to get this opportunity again after having come short in previous playoff attempts.

This time, it was James who wasn't the player with inexperience. He and the Heat had the necessary life experiences and skills to pick apart the OKC Thunder. The Heat won their first title since winning one in 2005 James would take his first steps toward shutting down the doubters as he won his first NBA Championship Title.

2012-13: Repeat

After winning a championship, a winning foundation was established. It was this foundation that brought in free agent Ray Allen. LeBron and the Heat acquired someone who could perpetuate their winning culture in the likes of Allen. Allen was a one-time champion with the Boston Celtics and was known for his thorough preparations for his games. He was the kind of building block the Heat needed to have an opportunity to repeat.

For a third time in a row, it would be the Heat that would end up the Eastern Conference Champions. Now, this was par for the course. The last obstacle that stood in the way of a repeat opportunity was San Antonio. The Spurs were back after a four-year absence.

The Spurs seemed like they had better pacing throughout the series. The Spurs and Heat were locked in a pattern in which the Spurs would win one, then the Heat. But in each of the Spurs victories, they held more poise, especially with their newfound three-point specialist, Danny Green. The series included a 36-point blowout initiated by Spurs team that set a Finals record for making the most three-point shots. Green scorched the Heat with 27 points.

With the Spurs in charge with a 3-2 lead, home court advantage didn't seem to matter, as James was in a position where his back was against the wall.

LeBron looked like a no-show this game. With 14 points tallied up in the first three quarters, writers and sports analysts were ready to lay down the criticism. Heading into the remaining bits of Game 6, doubt clouded LeBron's mind. The mathematical odds of coming back from a five-point deficit with such little time remaining were extremely slim. In the timeout huddle, LeBron looked like a lost man. The critics would be back at it again. LeBron would get the kind of backlash he has received for years. The stories of his inability to close in the fourth would come back to haunt him. It didn't help that he just threw away the ball in what could have gone down as one of the worst turnovers in his career. With the yellow tape laid out to prepare for the Spurs' championship celebration, it looked as if LeBron's fate as an incapable closer was sealed. Out of the timeout, only one thing was on the mind of the Heat team who were in a state of desperation. Down five, James heaved a three that would brick off the side of the rim. The Heat frantically scrambled for a second chance opportunity, passed back to James. This time he was able to knock down the three-point shot. Off the inbounds, the Heat fouled Kawhi Leonard. Chances were still very slim at this point. If Leonard hit his two free throws, the game would be back at a two-possession game, barring a miraculous four-point play to tie the game. Leonard missed the first and hit the second. LeBron had one more opportunity to save his Heat. From deep three-point territory, James missed a three and all hope seemed lost. It was at that moment; Bosh came up with an offensive rebound and passed it to Ray Allen who was back-pedaling for the three-point shot. Allen hit the shot to tie it up at 96. The momentum of the legendary three-point carried over into OT and the Heat made sure they would clean it up. An emotionally drained Spurs team couldn't contain the Heat, who played from behind during overtime. The Heat won 103-100.

The Heat knew they got away with murder. The Spurs lost a chance that was supposed to be locked up for them. Game 7 wasn't supposed to happen, but a miraculous sequence of events led to a final showdown. A dominating Game 7 from LeBron James would hush the critics. In a decisive fashion, LeBron scored 35 points, including a clutch basket in the fourth quarter to lock up their repeat title.

2013-14: 4th Year, 4th Trip to the Finals

The doubters were laid to rest. With two titles under James' belt, and clutch performances to back them up, James could focus purely on his legacy. The Heat surprisingly didn't make many off-season changes. This was a Heat team that narrowly came out with a title to an extremely deep Spurs team. They conservatively signed Greg Oden and Michael Beasley.

The Heat would take care of the season and head back into the NBA Finals once again versus a San Antonio

Spurs team looking to get revenge from their careless Game 6 from the 2013 NBA Finals.

This year's Spurs were a hungry team. With a 62-20 record under them, they looked like they were ready to take down the Heat. The Spurs seemed to engineer a defensive scheme exclusively to lock down the Heat. They would allow no mistakes like they did in the previous year. From top to bottom, the Spurs had an answer. Miami had no chance to win for the meticulously prepared Spurs. It was as if they were preparing all season to shut down the Miami Heat. The Spurs would go on to win in just five games. All their victories were won by at least 11 points. The improvement in Kawhi Leonard's game also was a huge factor in the gap between the two teams.

After the loss, James and the Heat were very accepting of it. Bosh pointed out to the media several times that the 2014 version of the San Antonio Spurs was the best team he has ever seen. If they were going to be okay losing to any team, it would be the Spurs. As for the never-ending criticism that rained over LeBron, reactions were surprisingly mild relative to previous times. It was a testimony to his winning years. His villain status had reverted back to being one of the most well liked athletes in the world.

Chapter 5: LeBron's NBA Career – The Decision 2.0

LeBron James was a free agent heading into the 2014 off-season and many thought he would re-sign with the Heat. There were always thoughts of going back to Cleveland, but why leave such a great opportunity to win more titles? However, the 2014 NBA Draft changed everything for Cleveland. Winning the first pick for the third time in four years, Cleveland could draft Andrew Wiggins, a top Canadian prospect who was hyped as one of the best players in the draft. The dreary city of Cleveland looked like it was going through a revival. With assets of potential at hand, luring James back to Cleveland seemed to be a possibility.

Return to Cleveland

After days of media hype speculating on the dream-like return of James, it was confirmed that James would be heading back into Cleveland. James made amends with owner Dan Gilbert and the fans in Cleveland were ecstatic to have their legend back in town.

A more mature LeBron humbly acknowledged the difficulty of winning a championship. As opposed to appealing to the fanfare like he did in Miami, there was no "Not 2, 3, 4, 5, 6" speech. In his open letter written through Sports Illustrated, his message showed that he's in it for the long haul. Through his four grueling Finals trips with Miami, James had a feel for what it takes to get to the top.

A few days later, the second wave of speculation hit Cleveland as they were in talks to acquire Kevin Love. The vision was to have a Big 3 of Irving, James and Love in Cleveland. The Cavs would have to sacrifice their future rookie, but with an enormous upside of potentially catapulting into being considered a championship contender.

A few weeks later, after the trade prohibition of Andrew Wiggins was lifted and the trade was official. The Cavaliers made more news in the basketball world as they followed through on the trade giving up their two Canadian picks, Andrew Wiggins and Anthony Bennett in return for Kevin Love.

The trade was in discussion for months even before LeBron came back. The arrival of James made Cleveland an enticing destination for Love and the green light was given by both sides.

The blockbuster trade officially capped the end of a hectic summer for James and his new Cavs team. Like many times in the past, the Cavaliers were back under the microscope as they automatically became labeled as title contenders. This marked a new era for James, who now faces the challenge of bringing a title for his home state.

The Return of the King

After months of anticipation, the Cleveland Cavaliers opened the 2015 NBA regular season at their home court against the New York Knicks on October 30, 2014. But, it was more than just a basketball game at the Quicken Loans Arena in Cleveland, Ohio.

Before the game began and amidst the thousands of fans who stayed outside the "Q" to welcome home their prodigal son, the full house of more than 20,000 fans greeted LeBron James with a thunderous ovation as the Cavs emerged from the tunnel. The sea of fans, which included Cleveland Browns superstars Johnny Manziel and Joe Haden, pop singer Justin Bieber, and R&B artist Usher stood on their feet as LeBron James and his teammates headed towards the bench.

As the opening tip-off neared, a brand new commercial from Nike featuring James, his teammates, and the entire city in a huddle was aired on the Arena's newly installed mammoth scoreboard. As the crowd continued to cheer, James watched the film clip from the bench and nodded his head in approval of the tribute and the adulation from the city.

It was a homecoming, an event, and a block-wide festivity combined into one. Unfortunately, the Cavaliers' game didn't live up to the hype around it— LeBron James played one of the worst games of his career, scoring just 17 points on 5-15 shooting and giving up 8 turnovers as the Knicks upset the highly favored Cavs 95-90.

The Cavs lost their season opener but that did not matter to the crowd, to the city of Cleveland, and to the entire state of Ohio. The more important thing was that LeBron James was back. And, James wasn't just back to reunite with his family and friends nor was he just plainly back in a Cavaliers uniform. He was coming back to fulfill the promise he made when he first set foot on the court: to win the Cavaliers' first NBA title. But moreover, James' return was seen as the first step in ending Cleveland's fifty-year drought of winning a professional sports championship. The journey had thus begun.

R-E-L-A-X

The following night, the Cavaliers traveled to Chicago where they faced the optimistic Chicago Bulls who, along with the Cavs, were considered the favorites to win the Eastern Conference. The Bulls had traded Derrick Rose and added Pau Gasol, Aaron Brooks, Nikola Mirotic and Doug McDermott to bolster their lineup. However, the night belonged to LeBron James who tallied 36 points, 8 rebounds, 5 assists, 4 steals and 1 block in a 41 minute battle that got the 2015 Cavs their first win of the season on the road against the Bulls.

But just when we thought that they had found their groove in Chicago, the Cavs lost their next two games on the road. First, Cleveland was pummeled by Portland with a score of 101-82, and then they lost a second straight game after Gordon Hayward hit a buzzer-beater that broke a 100-all deadlock. Suddenly, the highly fancied Cavaliers sported a 1-3 record, and it was already a hot topic of discussion for their detractors and a cause of concern for their faithful legions. But it wasn't anything for LeBron James, at least not yet.

The four-time NBA MVP took his act to social media and sent a reassuring tweet to the world: "In the words of the great @Aaron Rogers12 RELAX." James was referencing NFL quarterback, Aaron Rodgers', statement to frustrated fans after his Green Bay Packers started the 2014 season 1-2. The Packers won four games a row after Rodgers' declaration with Rodgers throwing 13 total touchdowns with no interceptions.

James' message was right on cue as the Cavaliers won their next four games to notch their first winning streak of the season. But instead of rolling, the Cavs lost their next four games by an average of 10.25 points with the star-studded team struggling in offense in those four losses with an average production of 89.5 points per game. Once again, the team didn't resemble the title-favorites they were touted to be before the season began. This time around, James sang a different tune.

I Stink

James had been critical of himself during the first month of the season, calling his game "passive", saying that he needed to assert himself more in games and admitting that he wasn't giving full effort. But after the four game losing streak, James went on to say "I stink" because he "wasn't doing his job". Added James:

"Me being the leader of the team, if I start hanging my head low then it's going to start going to everyone else. They look up to me. They look to me to make a difference and I've got to stay positive even through the rough times. As I've said before, this is not the darkest point that we'll see this year. I've seen dark and this is very light to me."

James was speaking from experience. During his first season in Miami, the Heat started the season 9-8 before going all the way to the NBA Finals. Although they lost to the Mavericks in the championship round, the Heat won back-to-back NBA titles after that defeat. Even the Roman Empire, great and grand as it was, wasn't built in a day. Neither were the Cleveland Cavaliers.

The Cavs were just 12 games in the season and with 70 games left to play, there was still an eternity of basketball left to be won. The struggles in the first month were expected birth pains of this all-new Cavaliers' squad. The Cavs had a new coach and a new system. They had a new go-to guy and a new core of players. Sure, this was not where their fans expected them to be at this point in the season, but this was not how they were going to end the season either—not with the best basketball player in the planet on their side. This team looked too good to fail.

Resting LeBron

Following that four game losing streak, the Cavaliers went on a rampage, going 13-4 in their next 17 games to improve to 18-11 going into December 28th. The Cavs went home on that date and played the struggling 6-23 Detroit Pistons. The Cavs were without Kyrie Irving who was nursing a bruised knee. The game looked like a routine day at the office with the Cavs leading by 15 points in the second quarter. But then the Pistons uncorked an 18-0 run to finish the first half and never looked back. Detroit went on to lead by as much as 27 points before settling with a 103-80 humiliation of the Cavs who were booed by their own fans.

James missed the next two games, including the game against the Atlanta Hawks on his 30th birthday due to a sore left knee. Three straight losses had pulled the Cavs down to 18-14 and in fifth place in the Eastern conference. The team then announced that James was "expected" to miss the next two weeks to rest the "strains" on his left knee and lower back.

In another twist to a tumultuous season, the team and their king seemed to be at odds when James said one day before the team announcement that he wasn't concerned with the injuries and that all the tests came back negative.

On the contrary, the Cavs said that James was examined by team physician Dr. Richard Parker at the Cleveland Clinic Sports Health and went through a series of tests, radiographs and an MRI. Dr. Parker advised James to take a two-week rest to heal his body. In addition to the rest, James was to be treated with anti-inflammatories, rehab and training room treatments.

At that time, he had played an extra 99 games from the regular basketball schedule in the last four seasons: 87 playoff games including four trips to the NBA Finals,

8 Olympic Games in London 2012 and four NBA All-Star appearances. During those four years, James missed just a total of 18 regular season games. In his 11 seasons in the league, he missed just 44 games. And when you think about the roles he played in all those games, all the bangs he took, the back to back nights, road trips and five night, four game stretches were beginning to come back to haunt him. He may have been the king, but he was not superman. After playing some 41,000-career minutes in the NBA it was time to rest his body and recharge his spirit. That didn't sit well with the Cavs.

Before the announcement of his "rest", the Cavs were 0-3 without LeBron James. They won their first game without him, a 91-87 victory over the Charlotte Hornets, but they went on to lose six consecutive games after that, including James' first game post-injury on January 13, 2015. That date would later become the most important game of the 2015 season for the Cavaliers as it proved to be the turning point of their season.

Trades That Turned Season Around

James came back from his rest re-charged and playing with a renewed spirit. On January 23, 2015 James scored 25 points, hauled up 6 rebounds and dished off 9 assists in the Cavs' annihilation of the Charlotte Hornets whom they had barely beaten two weeks earlier. James played just 27 minutes in that game because the Cavs had stormed out to a 40-point lead at the end of the third quarter. The final score was 129-90, their biggest winning margin of the year. The Cavs improved to 5-1 since James' return and then won five in a row. More importantly, James was starting to play with a lot of aggression. He was throwing windmill jams and was on the receiving end of half court alley-oop passes. He was starting to play some down and dirty defense. The Cavs were beginning to hum like a well-oiled machine, and more importantly, they were starting to win consistently. But it wasn't just because of LeBron James, although one could argue that his resurgence was key.

On January 5, 2015, the Cleveland Cavaliers acquired shooting guard Iman Shumpert from the New York Knicks in a three team deal that saw the Cavs trade Dion Waiters to the Oklahoma City Thunder. Shumpert was the perimeter defender that the Cavs had always coveted—especially since defense wasn't a forte for players, Kyrie Irving and Kevin Love.

Irving and Love's offensive prowess are well documented and Kevin Love is one of the league's top rebounders. But both do not have elite man-to-man defense skills and aren't as defensively sound as a LeBron James. So in a league where defense wins titles, the Cavs needed a defensive upgrade especially in the backcourt. Shumpert was the perfect choice.

But because the Knicks were cleaning up their roster at that time, they didn't just trade Shumpert. Instead, they packaged mercurial guard J.R. Smith in that trade to facilitate an obvious salary dump. The Cavs needed Shumpert and had financial capability to take in Smith's salary. So instead of worrying about the supposed excess baggage in Smith, Cleveland looked at it as the opportunity to acquire a pure three-point shooter.

Excellent three point shooters, Ray Allen, Mike Miller and James Jones, always surrounded LeBron James during his impressive run in Miami. James was able to lure Miller and Jones to the Cleveland fold, but Ray Allen had other plans.

The NBA's three point leader had skipped pre-season and told the public that he was unsure about playing again this season after his contract with the Miami Heat expired in the summer. But LeBron James was determined in getting Allen not just for his ability to hit the three point shot, but also for his leadership skills.

James knew Allen's game value because his three pointers in Game 6 of the 2013 NBA Finals saved the Heat's season and ultimately led to back-to-back titles. Yet it was Allen's championship experience with both the Celtics and the Heat that would've come in very handy for the Cavs who had key players like Kyrie Irving, Kevin Love and Tristan Thompson who have never played in a single playoff game. Ray Allen continually moved the date when he would decide where to play. James even met with Allen in Miami during his "rest" period but somehow, none of King James' advances worked on Ray Allen. He chose to sit out the rest of the season and left the Cavs hanging.

Spurned, the Cavs knew they were still one three-point specialist short in their line-up. Miller and Jones were there, but they have aged and are no longer athletic enough to do other things on the court. J.R. Smith was different. He possessed not just the three point shot but tons of athleticism that would make him fit with the Cavs offensive system.

Later that week, the Cavs sent the first round pick who they received from the Thunder as part of the Shumpert deal plus another previously acquired first round pick to the Denver Nuggets in exchange for seven foot Russian Timofey Mozgov. The Cavaliers had an eye on Mozgov even before the season began because the team needed a physical rim protector to perform at the heart of their defense. Mozgov's size and skillset were perfect for the job, and furthermore, he had previously played for Coach David Blatt in Russia. Secondly, the Cavs lost their only big, physical man early in the season when Anderson Varejao got hurt. They needed a replacement, and Mozgov fit that bill perfectly. The Nuggets really didn't want to part ways with Mozgov at first, but with the lure of two first round picks, they finally gave in to the Cavs' wishes.

So, in a span of one week, the Cavaliers shipped off a key player in Dion Waiters. However, they acquired three players who would later become important in their playoff run.

J.R. Smith's troubled history- on and off the court made a lot of teams shy away from him despite his basketball talent. His stint with the Knicks started off strong with the 2013 6th Man of the Year award but it had gone downhill since then, and the Knicks were willing to trade Shumpert out just to get Smith out of the Big Apple. LeBron James saw the situation differently.

"Get him here, and I'll take care of it." James told the Cavs before the trade. James argued that character wasn't the main issue with Smith. On the other hand, James believed that if he could sell the Cavs to Smith, J.R. could focus on the goal.

James' approval of the J.R. Smith inclusion worked like a charm; Smith thrived in Cleveland's free flowing offense and became their designated three-point hitter along with Kevin Love and Kyrie Irving.

Shumpert started his Cavs career on the sidelines with an injury, but once he returned, he played like he'd been part of the team for years. Mozgov was too familiar with David Blatt's system, and while he didn't have as much scoring power and flare as Shumpert and Smith had, his inner presence was silently making the Cavs' defense so much better.

Emergence of a Championship Contender

On LeBron's third game back from his self-imposed hiatus, the Cleveland Cavaliers visited the Los Angeles Clippers on January 16, 2015. Kyrie Irving exploded for 37 points to lead Cleveland to a 126-121 win and a second consecutive victory. LeBron James added 32 points, seven assists and 11 rebounds in another solid all-around performance. James topped the 30-point scoring plateau for the third straight time in his return but more importantly, he became the fastest player in NBA history to score 24,000 career points. That record used to belong to Los Angeles Lakers superstar Kobe

Bryant who achieved the feat at the age of 31 years and 75 days. James obliterated that record by scoring 24,002 total career points at the age of 30 years and 17 days.

Four more consecutive wins later; LeBron James was awarded his third Player of the Week award of the season and his 29th as a member of the Cleveland Cavaliers. It also marked his 49th time overall to earn that honor, the most by any player in NBA history. During that six game romp, the Cavs were winning by an average margin of 19.3 points while James was averaging 27.0 points, 6.0 rebounds and 6.0 assists over that period. King James was starting to dominate like he did in the previous seasons. The Cavs let him run the offense some more while letting Irving do much of the scoring and Love shoot the threes and grab the boards. Big performances came one after the other for James.

That six game winning streak would be doubled with the Cavs' 105-94 home win against the L.A. Clippers on February 6, 2015. The final score wasn't indicative of how the Cavs dominated the Clippers because Cleveland built a 32-point lead in the third quarter and allowed LeBron James to sit out the entire fourth quarter for rest. After the game, Iman Shumpert played the harmonica in the locker room while LeBron James put on a tight black T-shirt that was imprinted "RWTW" on the front. When asked, James said the initials stood for "Roll with the Winners".

At that time, no team was rolling like the Cleveland Cavaliers. They were starting to play well at both ends of the floor and LeBron James' stellar play was rubbing off on his teammates. The 12 game winning streak was their longest since 2010 and was one game short of the longest winning streak in franchise history. The 2015 Cavs didn't break that record as they lost to the Indiana Pacers 103-99 in their next game on February 6. But they had silently moved into first place in the Central Division after falling seven games down before the winning streak began. Cleveland also gained on the overall Eastern Conference standings, taking the third spot or going up two positions higher than where they began the year.

Strive For Greatness

On February 22, 2015, J.R. Smith and Iman Shumpert returned to Madison Square Garden for the first time since being traded to the Cavaliers. Cleveland won big 101-83 with LeBron sitting comfortably at the bench for most of the final stanza. James scored just 18 points in the blowout victory, but it was enough to put him past Allen Iverson in the NBA's All-Time scoring list with 24,368 points.

James started the season as the NBA's 25th All-Time scoring leader. Earlier in the season, he had also overtaken former Celtics center Robert Parish and then former MVP Charles Barkley in that list. Barely one and a half week later, James scored 27 points in

Boston to pass former teammate and ex-Celtics' star Ray Allen. On April 2, 2015, James would lead the Cavs to a 114-88 drubbing of his former team the Miami Heat at the Quicken Loans Arena in Cleveland. During that game, James' 23 points enabled him to move past former New York Knicks' big man Patrick Ewing and claim the 20th spot in the All-time scoring list.

James' march to greatness wasn't just all about scoring points; it was also about sharing the wealth on the basketball court. On February 24, 2015, James dislodged Chicago Bulls' forward Scottie Pippen for the most assists in NBA history by a forward. King James had 11 assists in their 102-93 win over the Detroit Pistons and that gave him a career total of 6,301 at that time or 7 more than Pippen had in his Hall-of-Fame career.

Scottie Pippen revolutionized the forward position. Pippen and Michael Jordan were the Bulls' primary playmakers instead of their point guard. During his prime, he was called a point-forward because of his ability to bring the ball to their floor and facilitate the Bulls' offense. For James to pass Pippen was iconic, because it was a tribute to his unselfishness as a teammate and greatness as a basketball player. On March 10, 2015, LeBron James also moved past point guard Mark Price to become the Cleveland Cavaliers' All-Time assists leader after dishing off his 4,207th career assist.

James would go on to finish the 2015 regular season with 6,302 career assists which is good for 26th overall in the NBA's All-Time assists list. Among the active players in the NBA, only Chris Paul and Andre Miller have more assists than LeBron James.

James' all-around brilliance continued as the regular season progressed and after its conclusion, James' Player Efficiency Rating of 32.2 broke the legendary Wilt Chamberlain's standard PER of 31.82, which the

Big Dipper set during the 1962-1963 NBA season. With that, King James now has three of the Top 10 regular season PERs in league history. Chamberlain also has three while the remaining four belong to Michael Jordan.

The Cavs went on to achieve a record 18 game home winning streak that helped them finish the season strong and put them back to the lofty title favorite status that was bestowed upon them during the preseason.

After a dominant run in the second half of the regular season, the Cleveland Cavaliers finished with a record of 53-29, which was good for second place in the Eastern Conference. They had completed a dramatic 360-degree turnaround from the Cavs of the past—a struggling 19-20 team that languished in the middle of the team standings in mid-January to one of the elite contenders that advanced to the 2015 NBA playoffs. From the starting point of January 15, 2015, the Cavs had a record of 34-9, which was the best in the NBA in that period. During that period, the Cavs had a point differential of +8.81 which was rivaled only by Western Conference leaders, Golden State, and the defending champions, the San Antonio Spurs who were the hottest team in the NBA coming into the postseason.

Chapter 6: James' Personal Life

LeBron, like many people in this world, juggles the daily struggle of raising a family. LeBron has three kids with his wife Savannah James. Not having had his own father in his life, he tries to pave a new path for his kids that he didn't experience; using the father-like examples he had growing up with Coach Dru, and his other mentors. A fact that LeBron frequently brings to the media is the challenge of not growing up with a father. In 2014, he wrote a public letter through his Instagram, about how he was able to be the man he was today without his father. It is clear that LeBron has spent a lot of time thinking about why he didn't have a father. Despite the fact that he takes pride in being raised by his mother, he makes it a priority to be there for his kids. Trying to raise his kids in the scrutinizing spotlight doesn't make it easy. Very few people can handle the lifestyle of being a basketball star, but LeBron, fully aware of his circumstances, tries to raise his kids to be as even-keeled and grounded as possible.

Chapter 7: LeBron James' Legacy and Future

LeBron will go down as one of the best basketball players of all time, without question. There has rarely been someone in the NBA who has possessed the same athletic talent as James equipped with a relentless work ethic and high level of humility.

James is also one of the fortunate few that have come away unscathed by the injury bug. Many high-caliber players like Grant Hill and Tracy McGrady weren't able to reach the highest peaks of their NBA ceilings due to their injury-prone bodies. However, it isn't all luck as James has made nutrition and his body a priority. James is often known for not taking his body for granted by fueling it with the proper nutrition it needs. Players like Dwight Howard have been known to overindulge in sugary goods and sabotage their bodies. In this regard, James' self-awareness is also what makes him one of the greatest to have ever played. The greats like Bryant undergo meticulous and scientific processes to take care of their body.

Another factor in why James will be recognized as an amazing player is because of his self-awareness of aging. Even the godlike James is aware of the aging process, and in response, he constantly adds elements to his game to prolong his years on the court. Self-awareness is an underrated trait when considering basketball legends, but it is often a key element in deciding who fits in the description of being an all-time great.

In terms of accolades, LeBron has a trophy collection very few can match. James is a 2-time champ with two Finals MVPs. He was awarded the MVP award four times in his career and is an eleven time NBA All-Star. James has been a consistent member of the All-NBA First team, appearing a total of eight times on the list. From 2009-2013, he was also on the All-NBA Defensive First team.

A great debate will always exist as to whether or not LeBron James is the greatest player to ever play the game of basketball. With many more years to go in his career, it's hard to say if he is better than other greats like Michael Jordan. However, LeBron has taken it upon himself to carve his own legacy as a consummate team player and intense competitor. It'll be exciting to see how his career ultimately unfolds.

Final Word/About the Author

I was born and raised in Norwalk, Connecticut. Growing up, I could often be found spending many nights watching basketball, soccer, and football matches with my father in the family living room. I love sports and everything that sports can embody. I believe that sports are one of most genuine forms of competition, heart, and determination. I write my works to learn more about influential athletes in the hopes that from my writing, you the reader can walk away inspired to put in an equal if not greater amount of hard work and perseverance to pursue your goals. If you enjoyed *LeBron James: The Inspiring Story of One of Basketball's Greatest Players* please leave a review! Also, you can read more of my works on *Russell Wilson, Kyrie Irving, Klay Thompson, Anthony Davis, Stephen Curry, Kevin Durant, Russell Westbrook, Chris Paul, Blake Griffin, Joakim Noah, Scottie Pippen, Kobe Bryant, Carmelo Anthony, Kevin Love, Grant Hill, Tracy McGrady, Vince Carter,*

Patrick Ewing, Karl Malone, Tony Parker, Allen Iverson, Hakeem Olajuwon, Reggie Miller, Michael Carter-Williams, James Harding, John Wall, Tim Duncan, and *Steve Nash* in the Kindle Store. If you love basketball, check out my website at claytongeoffreys.com to join my exclusive list where I let you know about my latest books and give you lots of goodies.

Like what you read?

I write because I love sharing the stories of influential people like LeBron James with fantastic readers like you. My readers inspire me to write more so please do not hesitate to let me know what you thought by leaving a review! If you love books on life, basketball, or productivity, check out my website at claytongeoffreys.com to join my exclusive list where I let you know about my latest books. Aside from being the first to hear about my latest releases, you can also download a free copy of *33 Life Lessons: Success Principles, Career Advice & Habits of Successful People.* See you there!

Made in the USA
Middletown, DE
28 June 2016